Releasing the Porcelain Birds

Also by Carmen Bugan

Poetry

Crossing the Carpathians (Carcanet/Oxford*Poets*, 2004)
The House of Straw (Shearsman Books, 2014)

Prose

Burying the Typewriter: Childhood Under the Eye of the Secret Police
(Picador, UK / Graywolf, USA, 2012)
Seamus Heaney and East European Poetry in Translation:
Poetics of Exile (Legenda/Maney Publishing, 2013)

Carmen Bugan

Releasing the Porcelain Birds

poems after surveillance

Shearsman Books

First published in the United Kingdom in 2016 by
Shearsman Books
50 Westons Hill Drive
Emersons Green
BRISTOL
BS16 7DF

Shearsman Books Ltd Registered Office
30–31 St. James Place, Mangotsfield, Bristol BS16 9JB
(this address not for correspondence)

www.shearsman.com

ISBN 978-1-84861-469-7

ACKNOWLEDGMENTS
Earlier versions of the poem 'Found in secret police records' appeared on the
Waterstones website and in the Oxford Magazine. 'Preparing for the journey
of return' was published in the Irish Times. 'The prisoner scribe's allowance'
was published in the Balliol College Record. 'Morning walk with Rosa' was
published in the Oxford Magazine. 'The house founded on elsewhere' was
published in the Shearsman Magazine. 'A walk with my father on the Iron
Curtain' was published in Modern Poetry in Translation. A large section of this
book was published in Big Scream.

I thank the Center for the Study of the Archives of the Securitate (CNSAS) in
Bucharest for giving me access to the archive of surveillance documents on my
family and for reassuring me that I can publish these documents. I also thank
my family for allowing me to publish the excerpts from our archive that appear
in the current book in my literal translation. The language of the translations
reflects the secret police-speak in the original files: I made no effort to correct
the grammar or improve the flow of the transcripts. I am grateful to Kelvin
Corcoran for his exceptionally sensitive, detailed, and careful editorial work
on this book. I thank my editor and publisher, Tony Frazer, for
publishing these poems.

Contents

For my father, on his eightieth birthday

I.

Found in secret police records

We are museums

We have now become museums. The inside of our souls
Was turned out like the lining of coats hung to dry,
And our souls have dried. Out of us came the warm breath
That you see when you blow on a window or in winter air.

Out of our footprints through the town, from the sound
Of us walking around the house they have made maps.
When we stopped at a shop window, the minutes were noted,
The address and what we looked at were kept on record:

The red dress on a mannequin, empty shelves in a bakery
On Hope, Victory, or People Street. Because we have become
'Objects of observation,' 'targets,' since nothing more has remained
Of the people we were, we are now museums.

On the ground level where we are closest to the earth, you will find
Our house with garden and fruit trees with sparrows, nightingales
And monarch butterflies. Then came the time of upheaval when birds
Were shooed from branches where microphones were installed.

The dog was poisoned by informers and the child was recorded
On a tape, when the electricity was on. The end of the girl's first love,
Her angry letters have rooms of their own, furnished with her mother's
Sympathy: maybe they were kept to indict us for having had feelings?

There are records of us eating sour soup and polenta, drinking linden tea,
Mother knitting sweaters at two in the morning to exchange for eggs
And flour; you will find her sitting on the bed 'alone by herself
Talking to no one for many hours,' framed forever in the state archives.

On the top floor, where we are further up from the earth, you will see us
Trying to escape: the girl asks her father to 'please talk about Kant,'
And he says, 'plan to live without me if I am assassinated.' We are
Museums. I am writing this down so you can come inside us to see.

There are no secrets anyway, everything about us has been recorded:
Night dreams and rage, irony and double-meaning, shopping we did
At the pharmacy, tears on our cheeks, even the illusion that
There might have been *something* we could have kept for ourselves.

February-April 2013

Found in secret police records

In memory of Seamus Heaney who believed that poetry can assuage pain

The dictator released the news of amnesty on his birthday
'To remain in history for his clemency,' Mother said
Not knowing it was her irony that remained preserved:
In our country people starved and friend informed on friend.

In his prison cell my father's jubilation was recorded:
'If I come out at the same time as any of you,
I'll buy a bottle of wine and some ham, that'll last us till home!'
The jailer warned him not to talk about what had happened there.

When Father came out of the train, the state archives say
He knocked on the door of old friends asking to make a call,
And I was the one who answered.
I sent him to Mother at work—she'd wanted to see him first.

(How she spent all the month's salary on stocking the fridge,
And worried about him traveling in the dead of winter
Wearing only his black suit, how she spat on the face of police
The morning of his release, when they asked her to inform on him.)

They walked in the door holding hands, his wrists raw from chains,
He caressed my brother, wanted to know what I have learned at school,
Then went around the house visiting each room; he asked for his shaver
And his radio, the night wore on. The antennae at the top of our house

Transmitted our feelings, the microphones must have blushed
At our words after long silence, the informer outside the window stood
At his post recording 'the atmosphere of joy on the part of children,'
Witnessing those first slow moments when I 'sobbed out loud
        uncontrollably'

Before returning to my senses. My father said to me, 'You answer
As if you are speaking on the radio,' and it was true. Records say

On February 5, 1988 we 'went to sleep at 3:45 in the morning,' Father
        'feeling
Tired, with a pain in his heart.' Snow fell, an angel dragging light.

*

Twenty-five years have passed. This morning snow arrives like butterflies.
I see us in our small kitchen that first night standing around each other
Not knowing what to say. The image disappears into these thousands of
        pages.
I no longer remember the pain in my father's heart. It was long ago.

Geneva, February 28, 2013

Releasing the porcelain birds

I found her porcelain birds today: three in one room
eight in the other, and those brought back to my mind
the one with the broken wing my sister and I once fixed

with Mother's nail polish and a matchstick.
The one bird with a broken neck Loredana and I hid
in the dog's cage outside, not to make her angry.

This is only a house inventory by meticulous
investigators: 'porcelain figurines,' they say,
'an elephant, a lion, a little girl with two puppies,'

and the birds, still around the ballerina,
among the 'crystal glasses and champagne flutes,'
the 'bottle of Slivovitz' (my parents' glamorous marriage),

their prized vacuum cleaner and Bulgarian rose perfume,
my father's 'seven shirts,' 'two colorful ties,' their
'tape recorder MK235 automatic Grundig made by Unitra Poland.'

'A black table with intertwined vine design,' and again
'three porcelain figurines (birds),'
'a wall library with two drawers and display case,'

'2 (two) hats made of light fabric and one leather hat,'
'3 (three) man suits,' 'a thick short coat,'
'4 (woman) summer dresses,' 'a violin and a guitar.'

My mother loved porcelain birds;
they must have made her think of flying
when such thoughts were banished

by men with keys to our house,
who chained her husband to the walls of prisons,
because his mind escaped to freedom.

'He represents a danger to our state,' a file says:
'Use all methods to monitor her, including special methods.'
'A radio Selena, a radio Gloria', 'display case with books for reading.'

*

How far you traveled my still swans, my white sparrows
archived for thirty years all over the country, shelved and cleared;
I see you now, when I am too old to take you in my hands

and run with you around the rooms of the house, or
place you on tree branches to see what the singing birds
make of you, to mend you when you shatter: as I did long ago.

A list of confiscated goods
and things destroyed by burning

We must have been hungry, since
my parents hoarded oil, corn flour, beans.

I was a 'minor' when they took the audiotapes
(with Christmas shows my sister and I put on

for Santa who joined us beside the tree,
Grandmother's frail voice telling us about her life

the summer before she died, our family songs).
I typed poetry. Parents drank whiskey;

they must have been unhappy: they recorded
Radio Free Europe transmissions, and typed

'We no longer need life and liberty':
they were ironical, cynical.

My father went to change the world with
wood, words, flags and a portrait.

The wood, words, flags and portrait were burned
(I imagine the fire at the secret police headquarters

in the center of their courtyard, soldiers
cleaning ashes, sweeping them under branches

of their chestnut tree: evidence seeping into
roots, dissent that must have grown into leaves

which even now continue to clap in the wind...)
The food was never returned to us. I still write poems,

about everything that was not planned to exist
once our photos were taken away with the food.

A birthday letter

The words 'the source informs you' echo in my head
that *other* voice—familiar, comfortable almost,

lining our private cries: 'the inmate wrote'
to his wife and children 'from the Aiud prison.'

Our letters journeyed through the clay-like
maze of secret police desks. Stamps, checks, dates,

signatures indicate officers and places. The paraphrase
of ongoing pain—half the time they paraphrased us.

That voice in introductions sticks to our words
like a skin disease impossible to cure. But then

some sentences from us burst free perhaps because
they're not translatable, editable, condensable.

They stand out in quotation marks:
unexpected missing heartbeats.

On 4 May 1985 my father thought about his birthday.
'Make a cake with fifty candles and take a picture.'

I recall the cake on our kitchen table,
and thinking about him in chains that day.

'My dear, the children are healthy,' Mother said.
'Come to see me with my children,' he said.

'Do you remember me coming home with snow
on my brow?' a letter says. 'Children, I so much miss you,

I kiss you all and your mother.' And me:
'How beautiful it would have been for you to have been here too!'

'Sell everything you can,' he urged, 'send the children to school.'
'Do not despair, I might be coming home soon.'

We hung onto those few words that could cross
the clay-like murky territories between us.

These letters were like skin that covered
and protected our bodies from the cold outside,

each word a capillary that carried and supported
the life in each one of us. Each word was limitless,

clothed our souls and warmed against despair,
shielded us from *their* world of terror,

transported chills, shivers, anger, warmth
from us to Father, and back from him to us:

they took us to each other as we were.
When the censor took our words and talked *about* them,

discarded our handwriting and wrote *his*,
he became a flaying instrument.

Letters we sent were not received
(until now, thirty years on).

We, Marsyas the Satyr tied to our tree.
The censor scraped at capillaries of our words,

what survives is howling: 'a year has passed with no news
from you'; 'something awful is happening to you';

'no one looks after us anymore, they're all busy';
'Mother is ill and short tempered, even Grandmother has left';

'it's disgraceful that you have nothing to eat.'
Thirty years have gone and we have lived

with exposed wounds, doubts, fears, uncertainties.
Now I find the family letters from back then

in the midst of thousands of records.
I reconstruct the way we used to speak,

the way skin used to feel when it was still alive.
Denatured letters in the handwriting of the censor.

*

I make out capillaries under the flaying instrument,
I reconstruct parts of the skin from the words

that were copied out. We now know
what has been taken from us and how

words alone saved us then
and bring joy now, the joy of finding them,   .

for in their frail syllables I recognize the old self.
Apollo has cleaned his instrument and left.

'BUTNARU'
at the visit with his daughter

The slash of sliding glass on glass at the window as
the guard prepared the microphone between us, when
my breath went from my room to his: *another* visit

comes to mind, but not *this* when I said that life is hard,
no wood for winter, no one to help,
school year finished well, and I aim to go to University.

This is a memory I no longer have:
aged seventeen, gone to prison to see my father;
all on my own, Mother was ill.

The transcript says the obj. (my father) rejoiced
in my visit—'the audience with his daughter'—he
asked for news from home, then told me his.

Father said (they say) was ill with nerves but
calming down lately, asked for medicines and then
announced that in the autumn he might come home.

He charged me with looking after Mother,
my little brother and working my hardest at school:
things will become easier when he returns.

*

Even today I do not dare ask him how
it felt then to look through the glass wall
and see a kind of freedom on the face of his child.

Two days on trains from our village to Aiud,
I wish I could remember what I thought,
if I was afraid to make the trip alone,

And how I felt about leaving him in that glass room
with his feet and hands in chains, my head full
of news to bring home to my ailing mother.

*

A quarter of a century without memory of this visit?
Now the handwriting of the officer on duty
calls me to the transcript with my name on it—daughter

of convict with a code-name: my grandfather's name
to be exact, probably used as mnemonic device
that linked us through generations across the country.

The record remembers what I no longer keep
in a self that I half-made with forgetting. Now the struggle
is between me and a piece of paper that talks about a girl.

*

The visit closes once again, dear life. I pray:
let it be as tender this time too, no crying, no hysterical
emotions, just pushing on and getting through.

And yet here's my father framed in his jailer's words,
our private sorrows like those of characters in plays:
at once my life and so removed from me.

My father, his jailer and I, a fine triangle.
Time on my side, I fling this stone of (rescued?) memory
into the river where you cannot step twice.

Transcribed from the Romanian Language

POST: 13JDER
No. Files: 2
NO: 0026124

                                        STRICT SECRET
                                        EXEMPLARY UNIQUE
                                        DATE: 26.10.1988
                                        INDICATIVE: 1/B.I.

Exploitation [illegible]
            'Barbu'

Hour 5:50 obj. and wife leave for work. At hour 18:10 wife
returns to domicile. After 25 min. arrives also the obj.
In the room we record the following discussion:

Wife: Where did you go?

Obj.: At Saftica. She will come by tonight. Everywhere I
went I was asked which roads I take when I return home. By
the railway tracks or by the main road, and what route I
take to go to work.

Wife: Oh, you don't say!?

Obj.: I will go to S. (his boss at work) and I will explain
this, and I will come home with the 5:30 (17:30?). What am
I to understand from this?

Wife: Only that they want to 'plan' something for you?

Obj.: If they want to 'plan' something, why should they
spread the rumours all around? To 'plan' something, you
work quietly..

Wife: This is so they learn your routes.

Obj.: To find this out, they could snoop around for a week
and...

Wife: Of course, you can only take this road to the railway
station.

Obj.: This is to terrorize me. That's what I suspect.

Wife: Yes, so you find out.

Obj.: Yes, so I will 'be afraid'. That's what I think. If
they wanted to do something, they wouldn't 'talk'.

[...] Maybe they want to get some hooligans to beat me.

Wife: Yes.

Obj.: They can bring their hooligans from Bucharest, theirs.

Wife: From today onwards we go together to the railway station. When you return from work, you walk with B. and I wait for you. Did you also tell S. about this?

Obj. Yes.
[...]

Their way

They are both old now, Dad turned seventy-nine,
I knew them mostly fighting with each other,
bickering like kids at school, playing tough.

How could I have guessed 26 October 1988
when she'd asked him where he'd been
and he replied, 'Everywhere I went

I was asked which way I take when I return home,
by the railway tracks or by the main road,
and what route I take to go to work.' 'Oh, you don't say,'

she said. 'This is to terrorize me. That's what I suspect.'
'From today onward we go together to the train station,'
she then said. What did she plan to do? Defend him

from murder with her own body? Shelter him from thugs?
They don't know I read this record, a quarter century on:
I am the link between their hearts, taking Love home

the way of words rescued from the state archives:
against forgetting, and against their silly parents' fights.
She stood sentinel for him at the station—and 45 years of marriage.

At hour 1:32

'At hour 1:32 we could hear someone trying the door that leads to the room equipped with listening devices.'

We always pretended to sleep, breathed regular deep breaths—as much as we could force ourselves—when their key clicked in our door.

'The door did not open, after which we could hear the footsteps of some-one going away, and the insistent barking of the dog as to a person who is a stranger to the house.'

After they left, we collapsed in leaden sleep. We woke up in the mornings with our heads pounding hearts tired of racing through the night, drank our linden tea in silence.

Then Father would take the hatchet from behind the stove and patrol the house, 'This is my house, no one comes into my house, or I'll kill him!' He'd wait with our key placed in the door so it couldn't be pushed out.

*

That's how he remained in my mind: guarding the door
from the inside, dog outside, poised to cry for help
to deaf neighbors, while shadows of hats and shoulders
crouched along walls for as long as nights lasted.

Transcribed from the Romanian Language   Strictly Secret
POST: 36 JCI   Ex. Unique
No. files: 1   Date: 26.10.1988
NO. 0023830   Indicative:
1/B.I.

To verify the legend
[Signature illegible]

                         'Barbu'

Hour 19:10, objective is called by B.

Cit. B: Where were you?

Obj.: Around at Saftica and the police station. Tomorrow
at 17 hrs. I need to be at… 1/B/I.

Cit.: M. (the relative of Cit.) was here, then at Galati,
and will come sleep at your house tonight.

Obj. Good.

Cit.: See that you don't close the doors, so you can hear
outside. They'll come earlier, around 19:30.

Obj.: Good.

…

Note of Explanation: --I mention the fact that this
conversation is a legend. There were other recordings
of this nature, to give the impression that the obj. will
have overnight guests. (Allusion to the presupposed ideas
of the objective that someone intends to make an attempt
against his physical integrity.)

… Transcribed–P.A.
27.10.1988

Legends

Who can tell a quarter of a century on if my father
was so terrified of sleeping in his own house

he arranged with relatives to receive phone calls
announcing overnight guests who never came?

Having guests in the house would have protected us
(logic implies): of guests we heard but did not see.

The secret police tapes say they recorded
legends, calls about things that did not happen:

Mother's sister asking Dad to keep the doors open
pretending to expect a cousin coming by.

Perhaps you're right, P.A., we were that scared
and though I don't remember this, it likely happened,

there were nights when someone stomped on the roof,
every tree had a shadow, and we couldn't tell

the real from the imagined. 'Tomorrow
I need to be at 1/B.I.,' my father is recorded saying

after his daily visit to the police station:
He could not have known that code-name

though I am certain he knew the *place* so well.
Your words, P.A., are in my father's mouth

and today it seems I read a version of ourselves
narrated in your own language that makes it

plain to see how you recorded and transcribed
our fears, how we lived without a choice.

Transcribed from the Romanian language   Strictly Secret
POST: 13 I.D.E.R.   Ex. Unique
No. Files 1   Date: 23.02.1988
No: 0026124   INDICATIVE 1./
B.I.

BARBU

At hour 22.00 the objective listens to the news
transmitted by the post 'Radio Free Europe'. His wife is
busy knitting. At hour 22:25 the objective attempts to
put Catalin to bed, by telling him a story with something
imaginary, the action taking place in the West, with a
life of plenty and without worries, a country with lemon
and orange trees..

Wife: . . . It's good also here with apples, and pears and
prunes. . .

Obj.: … I have been reading the magazine The World and
saw that 'there' in the developed countries the food
problem is something entirely banal, everything is easily
available
. . . So where is it better? There where you can find a
piece of good cheese or here with a piece of hard black
bread?

Wife: Also here is good!...

24.02.88
Transcribed: T.G.

'There'

The boy was five years old and he trusted
his father's stories about a life of plenty,

a country with lemon and orange trees.
'It is something imagined,' the records say.

'Apples and pears and prunes are also good,'
the mother countered (for the microphones?)

no doubt, tired of the hard black bread
the husband-prisoner brought to her.

But he went on imagining the blooms of
orange groves, endless summer trips

we were to take if not for real,
then in his stories with the action

taking place in the West,
itself a forbidden word

those days when we secretly cherished
his unstoppable rambling dream.

I sat in silence weighting apples, pears and plums
against mesmerizing gallops across distant prairies.

Transcribed from the Romanian Language Strictly Secret
POST: 13 JDER   Exemplary Unique
No. Files: 1   Date: 24.10.1988
No. 0026124   Indicative: 1/B.I.

                    'Barbu'
27.10.1988
Report urgently to direction to include these aspects
[signature illegible]

Hour 5:17 the objective's entire family wakes up. Among
the recorded conversations, the obj. tells Carmen:

'You must be very careful because you will be followed.'

Carmen: I don't care. If I could have been your lawyer at
your trial, I would have saved you from going to prison.

Obj.: I see. So you also understood that I served time in
prison for nothing.

Carmen: Of course.
[...]

Transcribed: P.A.
26.10.1988

October 24, 1988

According to the record number zero-zero
twenty-six-thousand-one-hundred-and-twenty-four,

that morning I woke up at five-seventeen and
made an affirmation that stirred police to action.

The conversation took place at post 13 JDER,
number of files 1, strict secret, only one record of it kept,

for the attention of 1/B.I. In other words
I was at home with my brother, sister, and my parents.

Were there really twenty-six thousand plus records
on us the year before we left the country?

There are *arrows* that mark my words:
I said to my father that I would have saved him

from going to prison if I could've been his lawyer,
he warned me about being tracked by them.

He seemed surprised I understood he served
for nothing, and sure of myself I let the 'Of course' slip.

To find such a record shining from the litany of blame
which then seemed just and also safe as self-defence.

Transcribed from the Romanian Language   Strictly Secret
POST: 13JDER   Ex. Unique
No. files: 1   Date: 12.07.1988
No.: 0026124   Indicative: 1/B.J.

'Barbu'

Hour 17:40 obj. arrives home from work. Once in the room,
he tells his wife: 'Carmen will not pass the entrance
examination to university. Not because she isn't clever or
is unprepared, but because she mustn't succeed. I know
their politics.'

Wife: That's all because of you. We did not want to tell
anyone where she was going to try, but in the end they will
find out.

Obj.: The moment you walk out of the door and get on the
train, the Securitate will be on your tracks.

Wife.: I'll know it if it will happen like this.

....

After this conversation they go out to do housework: the
wife in the kitchen, and the obj. in the garage.
...

Hour 20:30, obj. comes into the room and turns on the radio.
He listens to the news transmitted by The Voice of America
until 22 hrs.

In the room there is also the wife but no commentary about
the news is recorded.

Transcribed: P.A. 14.07.1988

A letter to 'P.A.'

I see now how you marked the day with ellipses
in the places where hours were allowed to pass

into oblivion: them working in silence
in garage and kitchen, after that transcribed conversation.

I would have liked to know what Mother made for dinner
and where I was, where my brother and my sister were

that night, you often mentioned these things—the coffee
and the drinks my parents had with friends, the laughter

in the room. But not on 14 July 1988. Did you know
I was to fail, as I did, the lists of winners and of losers

bringing me to tears, not knowing whether
it was me who failed the exam, or if it was an order?

'I know their politics,' my father said,
and Mother answered: 'That's all because of you.'

So many exams since, and one of them today
with magpies at the library window,

wisps of white clouds above Mt. Blanc,
this moving record that Father worried

and Mother pretended life was normal,
traveled far with me on that night train,

willing to pay with failure
for one necessary illusion.

Preparing for the journey of return
For Catalin

Do you remember the house, I asked my brother,
he was six and a half when we had left.

The grape vine trellis, he said, leading to the garage,
the right turn on the path toward the front door, the porch.

Are you afraid of what we'll see when we get there,
I asked my sister, and she said, yes, of the unknown,

because we're going where we haven't gone before:
inside our father's prisons, we'll see what no child should see.

Mother, I asked, since we left together we fought
illness and separation, loneliness and fears,

and we have embraced new languages,
starting from nothing in the middle of our lives.

Do you think this journey back will take us full circle,
will we find our old selves in our old house, do you

sense our roots pulling us back to the village soil?
It will be good to say good-day in our language, she said,

I miss the people and old streets, but home is now here;
today I cleared the yard and burned the leaves.

I asked my father, what about you, what will we find in prisons?
Suffering bathed in blood he said. And at home suffering bathed in tears.

And so we start from two continents, suitcases made and locked,
me with the maps of failure and dreams, rescued from police archives.

October 2013–February 2014

The prisoner-scribe's allowance

Walls are manuscripts and finished books, illuminated
With what the poet found in his cell: words of prayer
Snagged around the throats of rats, weaving the soul

With the spider's net, working its way in the darkness,
By the boarded window that only serves to remind him
Of the sky and air he could not let himself dream for.

Beware the dreams inside those rooms, they spring at you
For a clean kill: 'Punishment must be like this,' my father said,
'After all, you tried to change a country; don't dream in there.'

The guards do not give the prisoner-scribe a pen: that would
Turn the scribe into a man. He is left alone with the walls.
But what riches those walls, the souls of others spilled

Out on their cement face, their ghosts dancing in the shadows
Of the scribe's mind, material for books, four canvases wide open!
And forty-five kilograms of chains to turn into writing instruments:

The rust, the dried blood, here's the ink. He chooses the wall
By the invisible window and begins to write with the links of the chains
Moving his body around, etching the letters into the cement,

Until the first line comes out: 'Our Father who art in Heaven!'
He looks at his work, he has written over someone else's line—
He writes between another's lines 'Hallowed be Thy Name'

And beside another's, 'Thy Kingdom Come':
Then he illuminates the manuscript, now his nail is the pen
Ink the blood on his knuckle, he is instrument.

October 2013–January 2014

The prison committee's decision on 10.12.1965

Point 10: with respect to the nine points made above
(the number of days deducted against the number of days
added), 'the inmate Bugan Ion has to execute 3746 days of
incarceration.'

Signed: President, Secretary, Members (three)
          -signatures illegible
The Inmate (who signed below) was informed on 10.12.1965

3746 days

It must have been hard to tell
Monday from Tuesday, day from night
in a prison room with no daylight,

to sign this affidavit
that you'd stay chained to a metal cot,
no letters sent to you, no cigarettes,

just the howling of Time through
its own void. Standstill of seconds
minutes hours pushing against reason.

A prison to imprison an idea or a dream
is rooted in a country, continent, planet
and whirls out of control in a highway of stars.

Time stretched and crunched beyond the moon,
quantum foam, stardust, the cosmic ray
that comes right through cement walls

from the Universe to him, pencil in hand,
signing his own sentence by which atoms
of his own blood, particles smaller still

will be born from the combustion of his mind
racing beyond the speed of light: Time has
no meaning, you can force it like

breath through a trumpet, it comes out
the other side as music. Three thousand seven
hundred and forty six days left to rot

in the company of rats, inmates' howls
through days and nights, hunger, insults,
knowledge that the world outside lives on.

March 20, 1965:
File of Certification for Transfer of Objects

The undersigned Lieutenant Colonel C. Z. of Military
Unit 02866 Constanta handed in and Major A. I. from
the Regional Section M.A.I. , received the following
documents and objects:

1). 1 (one) protocol (certificate) of area search
comprising two files and an annexe of 4 (four)
photocopies;
2). 1 (one) tourist rucksack;
3). 1 (one) binocular case;
4). 2 (two) woollen blankets;
5). 1 (one) shaving razor;
6). 1 (one) shaving brush;
7). 1 (one) shaving paste;
8). 1 (one) battery 4.5W;
9). 1 (one) lighter;
10). 1 (one) coin of 3 lei;
11). 4 (four) coins of 1 leu;
12.) 6 (six) coins of 5 bani;
13.) 2 (two) coins of 10 bani;
14.) 1 (one) English-Romanian dictionary;
15.) 1 (one) German textbook-12 pages long, in deteriorated
state;
16.) 3 (three pieces of cotton for wrapping the feet);
17.) 1 (one) beer bottle that contains 50 ml of medical
alcohol;
18.) 17 (seventeen) half-slices of hunters' salami;
19.) 2 (two) thin loaves of bread;
20.) 1 (one) screwdriver.

The aforementioned objects belong to escapees Bugan
Ion and P. T. who crossed the frontier from the People's
Republic of Romania to the People's Republic of Bulgaria
on the day of 21.02.1965 hours 23:35 between the points
110-111.

No objections were made to this transfer.
Concluded today 20.03.1965 in Constanta.

From the UM 02866 Constanta
Lt. Colonel, ss/Z. C.

From the Dobrogea regional branch M.A.I.
Ss/Mr. A. I.

A walk with my father on the Iron Curtain

Arm in arm, my father and I return
to the ground of his failed escape:
it is now forty-eight years on.

The border between Romania
and Bulgaria at 110-111 point
is bathed in gold October light.

The corn silos where he slept are still here:
an old border guard curious to see us
loitering on the train tracks confirms Dad's memory,

as if History itself sent him our way
with the flock of geese and the red tractor
raising all the clamor in the peaceful morning.

It's a holy day for me, at my father's side,
with the map of his life, listening, listening
to the tempest in that night, icy rain, snow,

him and his friend inside the corn shelter
melting snow for tea, the horrifying days
when they searched the way with binoculars.

He ran to the other side of the world
with seventeen half-slices of salami,
a flashlight, and a dictionary,

some coins, probably more for good luck
than for anything they could buy, the shaver
for good looks, and a heart full of hope.

We carry on past Negru Voda:
Tolbukhin railway station, golden afternoon
and a wind that buffets us,

then Elhovo that looks more like a painting
with a dream worked inside the peeling blue
walls of the train station, my father, a puzzle

in changing light, seen through broken windows,
the coffee and baklava on the main street.
Arm in arm in the old quarters searching for his hotel

where he hid from police, the trap door that is
no longer there. Memory leads us off the map.
Then Lesovo in fog, like an elusive fish, the map

with the haystack where he slept to hide
from border guards, his hike along the roads
through the circular swamp, 400 metres from Turkey!

Ground of being on his ground of escape.
You cannot take the dreams away from anyone who dreams.
'I never thought I'd be back here as a free man,' he says.

Here he is, the white in his hair, snowbells at temples,
the grey-green eyes, now wet, now dry, twinkling.
Locals watch us step off ghost trains at the disused station.

II.

Life without a country

Life without a country

Things have been laid inside us.
Stored, layered with the clay and clean water.
Stones of peaches stood for what was lost.
I am a slice of earth opened by the road.

We cut through chamomile fields
I only remember this morning for the first time.
A glance in the early hours over the field outside the village
Brought the girl I once was
Running over a black snake on a rusty bicycle,
The bump over the shiny body that curled into itself.

That first solitary trip into the wide world
That made the return so scary,
Made me search for another road back.
This is the other road back,
Through time and through other countries.

Everything has now been opened
And the fresh air already dries the sediments of the earth.
The train behind the cemetery,
The deer painting that we left to my cousin Costel,
Our kitchen rug in *Tanti* Saftica's back room,
The birds made of horns my uncle lacquered,
Glued to little stumps of wood, and gave as presents,
My childhood adventure books, Jules Verne,
Novels of adolescent escape
From a life with the secret police.

Stolen pain.
Robbed intimacy.
Our story.

Balzac, Dumas, Dickens, Stendhal startle
From *Bunicu* Neculai's house where my cousins placed them
For safekeeping.
Invisible roots left and forgotten,
Breathing when you find and touch them.

Mum, Loredana and I are in church: we pray and cry. Images from our past settle among icons and chairs, over cushions and in the light of candles. My life began here with prostrations and the laughter that comes over children who admit to all the sins, whether they committed them or not, and not giving a thought to prayer any more, go straight out to play. My best friend's mother grabs my hand and waits for me to recognize her. I have been searching for Aurora for twenty-five years but I never returned to our village church to find her mother. My parents' lives began here with their marriage one August when my grandparents' garden was full of flowers.

*

We have returned from an improbable future fifty-two years after my father first tried to leave our country. Police guards make visitor badges for my father, mother, brother and sister, and for me. They place them on our chests, so we can be cleared as we walk into our father's prisons, then next to the passport booth that once used to be the Iron Curtain between Bulgaria and Turkey. My brother has become the camera and the camera is him. To the people who came to church this Sunday my mother, my sister and I might well return like a lost arm, or like a nightmare from the past, or ghosts, reproaches.

Our country has lost its memory.
The bus is our capsule.
We are transported into our new lives,
Out of the world we loved, we hated and abandoned,
And tried to forget. This has been only a twelve day trip.

Cats, horses, smoke of autumn leaves, wells, people in their yards.
The two wells my parents dug at the edge of the woods outside the village,
Lifeline for others, memories for them who have drank
The freedom of exile
But not the water they brought to the surface.

We drive on and out of our village still talking about the prayers for our dead in the cemetery. The flowers we spread on the graves—chrysanthemums—bagels and lit candles, traditional towels, a bottle of wine that the priest emptied on the headstones and earth of *Bunicu* Neculai, *Bunica* Anghelina, *Bunica* Ortansa, while Loredana and I sang 'Vesnica Lor Pomenire' with the Priest, and Mum cried.

    Sitting by their graves in the wind of this October, squinting in the sun, with the train whistling past and the song of birds, grave diggers throwing the fresh earth on the path, I can't tell if we are the ghosts or if the souls in the graves are coming out to sing to us. I don't know who has been dead all these years. This is the only place on earth where life and death seem right and I don't want to put up a fight against any of them. This is the only place where I feel my sense of identity physically, in the pit of my stomach.

The driver presses on and we leave behind
The smoke of leaves in the sun,
Stacks of cabbages and quinces on porches and by the roadside.
Our relatives disappear from the rearview mirror.
Their words in *our* language stay with me like that warmth
You find inside the lining of your coat when you slip
Your hands inside it in a cold train compartment.

A dream of return

We have now returned to the source of our selves,
our country of birth, our house, and drunk

the final dregs of tears from our past.
Drank also from the source of joy, grandparents' well

that we made holy with our memory from the solitude of exile,
brushed the chipped cement from its rim, and wiped our eyes.

One rainy day we prayed at the old icons of our church,
walked again through the doors of the village school,

found the graves of our family in the small cemetery by the railway,
shook the hands of those who could still remember us.

History marched over and left behind the evidence
of how our selves were torn from us:

we found thousands of pages with stamps, signatures,
typing and handwritten notes by informers, us—

objects of observation—lieutenant colonels, majors,
neighbors and friends, passers-by declaring what they saw

of our resistance, stubbornness, pain. Dossiers and files
bear our names and code names, separations, secrets.

We huddled over our maps of dissent, maps of escape,
trekked each one of them, then held the map of exile.

*

And here we are this morning, flying back to our nowhere,
lighter for having left our past behind for good.

Time has turned on our side now, we fly together
with our old selves, carrying our old sorrows, at last.

19 September 2013

The fourteenth spring

This season God sent you a bird's nest on the porch
with three little blue eggs and a busy robin
waiting every morning outside the door to sing to you
of life's joys in the heart of loneliness.
I remember fourteen springs ago when I knocked
over the nest and spilled the tiny eggs in the garden
as I planted irises to take my mind off the doctor's news
and everything else I knew would await you.
Here is a photo of you with the chicks this morning:
Mother says you spend your days on the porch
feeding them cherries. St. Francis giving thanks,
and me thinking of you, and the saint, and of giving thanks
all the way from here where I cannot touch
your old, smiling face that delights at the birds' song.

The clocks of our birthdays have been turning,
we stand together still inside life's great circle
blessed with blue bird eggs, of robins? Hard
to tell from the picture, harder yet for you to know
the names of birds in English. We almost miss
the real thing for not naming it, like I almost
lose touch with your face by not being there. Yet
not quite! Days, delight and love are all still here:
Mother looks at you with the camera to send the image
all the way to me. I see you both, and the birds.
Maybe that's all there is: the almost missing
and the almost touching life.

May 2014

III.

The house founded on elsewhere

The house founded on elsewhere

He who turns against his language, adopting that of others, changes his identity and even his deceptions. He tears himself—a heroic betrayal—from his own memories, and up to a point, from himself.
　　　—Emil Cioran, from *The Temptation to Exist*
　　　　　(translated from Romanian by Carmen Bugan)

I.

Today is allowed to exist and then vanish
Like the seagulls and their shadows on
The still-seeming water in the Bay of Bantry,

Where I walk unnoticed, unrecorded,
Making memories of compass jellyfish swimming
Up with the tide, after the storm, to the beach.

My own shadow, stooping, standing
Over rocks and sand, back on the walking path
Simply means that I exist, and there is light.

That is all that will remain of today, no official record
Will testify against what I say that I see. As for me,
I hover in the space between the seagull and its shadow

Loose like a thought that tries to cling to something,
To celebrate the swans and their mirror image,
That medusa that opens like a flower in the sun,

Green lobster nets and masts of boats
Writing something oracular on the horizon
For those who are without a home.

II.

The first crack appeared on the ceiling:
Thin like the shadow of a spider's thread
Cast along the crease where the walls merge.

No one other than her noticed it there.
She couldn't take her mind off it, the way it
Stood in her view as she looked out at mountains

Between trees from her place at the table:
It brought a subtle wrinkle on her face.
Later on a larger fissure appeared, the paint

Swelled like the skin below the eye following
Sleepless nights, plain to see above the table.
She set to mixing cement, took out

Smoothing instruments, drained the weeping wall
And mended until all looked well again.
She built the new house with words bought

At the price of exile, letting memories go astray,
Fall where they may like dust.
How many times she walked around the rooms

Anxious and proud that she made it all with a translated
Prayer, a new version of the old prayer, holy
Oil from elsewhere, rituals and superstitions

From elsewhere, but all renewed and changed
Again, four languages over, where they show
Why they could pass through words that changed her.

III.

When the walls became full of cracks she knew no words
She cemented would last unless she uncovered
The foundation of elsewhere on which her house was built.

She dug around it, moved the earth little by little until the old stones
Showed through: porous pain, old fears, mistrust. She placed
Next to them what she could find around: a bit of happiness, a bit of fear

A little bit of courage. All in the language where she
She learned them. Cement now, water, patience,
Piece by piece the foundation is renewed.

She looks at her children and husband. She will mend this wall
With words from here and elsewhere and let them
Help her build, rebuild and fix: their common love and skill

Should outlast time, be stronger than her will alone.
They play-build like when she was young and poured the foundation
Of that first house she cannot forget: the childhood house of joy.

IV.

Stefano is three years old, he fills his shirt with pears
And runs: 'Mommy look, what shall we do with them?'
I take out the camera and rush to him, his soft cheeks,
Busy little hands, his golden curls. The grass is full of pears.

V.

Alisa puts her arms around me: 'Come play with me!'
She runs around the room with her bare little feet, here, there,
Like a sunray that escapes through wind-blown trees
In summer's day and lights up unexpected places.

VI.

It is the lucid sky after the wind
Has swept the debris that has come from far away:

Cirrus clouds like torn night shirts
On the shoulder of the Jura whitened with first snow.

All clean now wherever you look, lit by the coin of the moon.
Turning to the second half of life,

Knees grazed against the web of splintered light.
And here it comes, a word at work through those fallen notes:

The touch that brings on all other touches
With the rightness in them, turning and moving again with you

The moonlight sonata in my ears in morning sun at the desk:
Different this time, a new kind of music, awake, luminous.

VII.

Not all the words you say are the Self and not all turning
Against your language is self-betrayal. Behind each word
Is what tries to get inside it. That is what matters

Whether I speak it in my own language
Or in the tongue of others. The thought, the breath
With which you send love out, or forgiveness, say,

Outlive the words and languages, outstrip
The syllables at prayer or play. I speak of smiles and tears
And better yet, smiles through tears at the end of day.

And so the house stands with what it can:
A sagging wall, a brand new door through which
Come children with schoolbooks and street-side flowers;

Solid enough to face the winter wind and baking heat,
Each word inside for what it's worth and what it can say:
Good enough to bear the weight of what's to come.

June 18–July 10, 2014

Light

This Sunday's rain blew in from the mountain
straight into the fruit at the market,
a wet kiwi in my hands like your unshaven face,

swirling leaves landing on red apples.
Up above the rooftops a finery of rain light
and sunlight, handsome half-ring, rising.

I ran towards the rainbow
certain that if I touched it my skin would be painted
with its shimmering light. The white clouds

behind it seemed stained with colors,
the blue shirt of the sky soaked; me too—
I wanted to bring you the rainbow on me.

The sun went behind a cloud and the colors
began fading: you must see it when it scares you
with its light, makes inside you the other half-ring.

10 November 2013, Geneva

Sete

The wind gusts move like the flexing muscles
of a hunting animal.

No: the wind blows on the tongue of sand
and flattens the beach grass.

The two of us crouch,
children in our arms.

Miles of stinging heat abrasive sand:
but the reward is tinted seashells like we have never seen.

Rosy stones, a white medusa, squeezed lemons
at the bar next to the *Poste de Secours*

and learning to trust our weight to the wind—
walking backwards, arms in the air,

children shouting songs to sea and sand,
twirling this way and that.

Narbonne

From a stone-shaped, sandy, wind-swept
landscape filled with vineyards
rises the gothic cathedral of Narbonne,
a compass guiding us away from heat.

Here and there a chateau ensconced among trees,
rows of vines drawing whatever sweetness
from arid hills, palms along the road
and glimpses of sea around the bends.

The next day everything is on fire:
palms, the vineyards, trees, roadside grasses,
and we, unscathed, drive through cinders
after the helicopters and trucks have drowned the flames.

We speed by the last burning tree,
dry wind blowing through the now-thin smoke,
our candle offerings having already given their thanks
in the heart of the unfinished cathedral:
this year's communion wine will smell like the wrath of nature.

Perpignan

On the way to the dressed-down, languid Catalan-French town
with the gypsy quarter full of happy children
sitting on the steps, its cathedral 'a masterpiece of southern gothic'
and narrow streets threaded with flags and wind-breaking nets,
we drove through a thunderstorm:
a full tree branch landed on the road making us swerve,
the wind turned the windmills, buffeted the car,
fattened the orange warning flags that blew sideways.

It was quiet on the way home, the sun burned,
we brought back images of city walls and convents
built with golden river stones and red brick—Roussillon ochre,
the *Palais des Rois du Majorque* speeding past us,
the tourist train driver who talked with everyone in town
as he whirled us around the narrow, crowded streets.
Gone now the menace of the storm, gone the wind
like a ghost we imagined. Our car is filled with postcards
and maps of places to visit—next time around.

Cap d'Agde

There is a road from Beziers to Cap d'Agde
that is lined with sycamores, trimmed
like soldiers at their posts, following the river
with the nine locks one on top of the other:
we took it to escape the heat and wind
that scalded the motorway.

Lush green clumps of trees, vineyards,
a village church next to the river, and us,
children singing in the car (they always sing).
When we arrived at the old port of Cap d'Agde
that hangs above the sea, people like lizards
were lying on flat stones, past the bushes,
baking in the sun. My white scarf took off
in the wind. Some plunged into the sea
and swam toward the moored sailboats,
children caught algae and mussels between the rocks,
and music came in gusts from restaurants
following bare-breasted women with dark nipples.

We waited half a day in the shelter made by rocks
collecting seashells and stones,
until the tide began to move our slippers from the sand
and the sun lowered its glare enough for us to come out
for a swim—Stefano still carrying his net full of mussels,
Alisa's dress filled with white smooth pebbles.

The Mediterranean

Eucalyptus and palms, cliff drops that slice the sky
Into the azure of water, salt that sticks to the lips,
My children's first sea, their first medusa, sudden waves.

The Mediterranean changes her faces from morning till night
But none of her blues speak to me. (I console
Myself now with the glacial lakes in the Alps—Annecy—

And memories of waves of another lake
That helped heal, and stirred the water behind my eyes
And laid out sands and forests where I found repose.)

*

Children wash on the shores of Lampedusa in little lumps.
Mothers flee bombs, seek the promise of a dream
For a better life, and end up fattening the fish.

At *Les Calanques* near Cassis the Captain says, 'prepare
Your cameras: capture the nesting cormorants on the rock pillar,
Then look down, the bottom is far deeper than it seems.'

I gaze into the hypnotically clean sea,
A blue I cannot describe, shimmering blue fish
Dances in vertiginous perfect water. Back on land

I see people who escaped and now are
Tongue tied in the arms of life, whatever that is,
Dragging memories behind them like sacks of stones,

Forgetting the breastmilk of their native tongues,
Staring at hard faces who say they are unwanted:
Vacant, spent, and resigned in the sea of freedom.

August 2014–November 2015

The porcelain birds have escaped
from their imagined rib cages
and cracked their rigid wings into thousands white pieces.
Souls slid through the frozen beaks and eyes.
Out of timelessness they move through the air,
Inexorable, and light.

*

Far away, on the TV screens,
far off on the radio waves,
wars are being fought:
children are murdered in schools,
mothers cradle dead limbs in their arms,
fathers close their fists and open their hands
to carry coffins full of severed dreams.

*

I am in a room full of windows
with the sun in my heart,
death stalks. The rose of the breast
will be opened like a lid
in the next hours, and I have asked
to stay wide-awake until the very last minute,
when they will fill my veins with sleep.

Morning walk with Rosa

In memory of Jon Stallworthy who nurtured till the end

You have to be there at the moment when
The sun works with the milk-thick fog
And both of them are paper-white light.

Things as they are no longer seem the same,
You stand in the field, inside the foot of a rainbow
Looking at fog lifting through the rising sun.

Millions of glistening droplets float by
Leaving your cheeks wet, hair humid
And your breath snagged on a 'spider-made-star'

As Rosa whispers, 'étoile.' So that is what's under the fog:
Spider-made stars. Perfectly symmetrical webs
Of fine silk-like threads hanging on blackberry bushes,

Late pink baby roses, between leaves of trees,
From stem to stem and every branch. And now
The sun turns slightly golden and I see

Delicate parachutes landed between ravaged
Sunflowers' stalks, domes of white sky-light
As if the field is lit up by a thousand white lamps.

The spiders have worked with the fog: their nets
Are clad in tiny droplets, minuscule pearls, diamonds,
Disciplined, in perfect rows hanging to the threads

That have followed the shapes of leaves, for now
We are looking at trampolines made of spider webs
Drizzle-plaited, finished off with pyramid-like tops,

And here come the double, triple layered iridescent sheets
Of honey-comb-like structures swaying to our breaths.
Then back to spider-made-stars

That flutter in the air holding their glitter
Up in the open fields, half green, half brown.
I have never seen so many nets carrying water light.

October weaves her tapestry on grasses,
Nets on trees, and we run fingers along translucent
Threads to collect the water on our skin,

Touching the miraculous. So much to see
In the fog, as in the last days' sadness.
The richness that's around seems deeper

When you didn't know to look for it, and saw it there
As fog's offering—a path full of shimmering stones
To help you find your way when you can't see ahead:

The spider web that hangs to the mailbox
Drawing your mind away from the letter,
Into its calming inner architecture

That depends on just one kind of warmth
Born of a sudden morning chill that makes the vapour rise
From mounds of leaves, and fog breathes rainbows.

Here 'étoile', star, is a play on the French 'toile d'araignée'
October 14–November 12, Prevessin-Vesgnin-Ornex-Moens

Walking with Martine

'You were not lost on that poplar path,' she said turning into the lane between the houses of Vesegnin: 'That is *L'Allée du Château* I used to take to school riding my bicycle sixty years ago. They built their garden fence right beneath the trees and had the cheek to put up the Private Property sign. The stuff that people do these days on public land!'

The row of poplars stands in the autumn sun like a past glory and I see Martine the girl fast on her bike cutting through the fields, wearing (I am sure it must have been) her red dress, as she nearly sprints to show me what's left of the village. I found in her what I wanted: someone who aged with a place, a companion for my solitude these mornings when it's hard to see ahead.

'Look how these folks have planted their bushes on the road just to gain another half a meter of green, you'd think someone might want to look into this; ohh, they dump their disused doors outside their garden fences, the world has changed.' We cross the fields she calls the 'green way' which in the summer were filled with storks and hawks, goats and cows and their bells.

In Ornex she shows me the one standing farmhouse behind the new Peugeot garage: 'That was where I was born, the new owners have kept the stove my daddy built, and the stonework on the outside. All around were fields, we must have been five-six houses here, and the rest, forests. They cleared paths through woods so we could walk to school.' And then she turns to apple trees, and cows, and greets the cats on fences walking with the *gravitas* of one who knows each flower pot in the village, the families who stayed and those who left, when the bread at the bakery stopped being good, and when the butcher's family had left and the new butcher came in with his children, and his wife and his homemade sausages.

Every morning I wait for Martine in her red walking suit, for her grey-blue eyes to sparkle with anticipation of the walk, and I follow her along hidden pathways, between garden gates of walled-up houses; behind the cornfields that surround one village and lead into the next; under pear trees that drop their fruit on us; next to laden apple trees; by patches of cabbages and pumpkins with their bellies in the sun. The air is full of birdsong and cowbells. A sycamore stands alone in a field of sunflower stalks: it grows as we walk toward it from the stream and when we are under it we see Mt. Jura rising.

Martine bends to move the snails out of the way, places slugs back on the grass with her stick, curses at a stray coffee cup littered by a bench, drags the broken branches of the walnut tree off the path to make the walk safe, forever cleaning up after the rushing world, delivering just grumbling when needed, and humming to herself when we pass by the rolls of golden hay, 'Ah, c'est jolie, n'est pas?' she says, and I agree, 'Cette promenade, une belle souvenir pour moi.'

Crossing the woods with Dennis

It's eight-thirty on a September morning and he stands by the front door next to Martine and Rosa, waiting for me with his walking stick, sunglasses, and the instrument that will measure the time and distance we will make today; trajectory, the natural reserve of Meyrin, ancient village of Mategnin, sunflower and cornfields on the border between France and Switzerland leading to the woods and farms between the checkpoints.

This is one of my favorite walks for it zigzags inside the thickness of the border and we always go without passports, being what we are: *frontaliers*, creatures of frontiers, carrying earth from one country to another on the soles of our shoes. He stops at all the mud puddles in the woods to look for frogs with his stick, and moves easily along the deer paths as if he were a hunter. They all discuss which way avoids the roads, the best lane to the farm that sells asparagus, they taste peas in a field.

We wander under the canopy of arches deep into the woods that lead to fallen trees and thick thickets, magical and quiet as if no one ever walked into them. The air is opulent with leafy smell, humid earth, clearings release grassy sun-warmed currents that go up my arms making me giddy. Then comes Mategnin around the bend of a road lined with sycamores: first a farmhouse restored, a huge garden with strayed-about white chairs and geranium pots spread on lush grass. At the village fountain we drink above a rectangular stone vase from the mouth of an iron lion. The village green is a small circle around one tree with two benches under it. That's all Mategnin is, about seven-eight houses that were kept with all the ancient stone in them and have geraniums on all the small square windows peering out into green fields.

On the way home, through the village of Prevessin, Dennis looks at houses and points to his wife Rosa those he'd like for himself: the one with the wood for burning stacked all around the walls, or the one with the antique cart (as in horse-drawn cart) near the swimming pool, which, he observes, is well-placed behind the rosebush hedges so it looks like a lake. Or the big house that would have place for his whole family, his mother too—who scolds him for reaching beyond his means, though he doesn't really crave the richness of those mansions, he only dreams aloud to pass the time. And so we're on our way, me with my cartload of unfulfilled dreams and the jacket pockets full of walnuts Rosa gathered from the walk and offered as a gift; a gift of the road, the three of them richer than they will ever know.

Through the village streets
For Stefano

All of a sudden it seems you read:
The street sign that we passed by all these years ago
Today says in your boy's voice,
Fin de zone 30, Prevessin–Moens,
Our street opens up to you the rights-of-ways.

Your hand is nearly as big as mine now;
We exchange gloves to mock the winter wind,
You leave messages for me written in
Letters that straggle off the words like children
Standing in a crooked line. You read what I write—

A hurried letter (Dear Lucy…) stealing that silence
From me, when I am alone with the paper.
Suddenly it seems, you read,
And I remember your first smile drunk in breast-milk,
The moment when you looked into my eyes,

The first time when you recognized me in a crowd,
That one day when you laughed for the first time
Because something was funny, and we wrote it down
So you can find it later, when you're grown.
But now you read, and with you I take all words as true.

Is this window ours?

For Stefano

Which window? I ask holding his hand
As we walk the length of our rented apartment.
'This one that looks at the mountain,' he says
And then turns, 'And this wall, Mummy, is it ours?'

'Nothing is ours,' I smile to him, myself
Now used to the sunny almost empty rooms,
That we un-cluttered in order to make more space
For him to breathe better.

We play this game so often, and when he asks me
To buy the whole apartment, with walls and windows,
The light bulbs and the cupboards, I don't know
What to say, except, 'There will be other windows

That will show us other things, don't worry about owning
One. In having none we have all of them:
Like countries and like languages.' 'Yes, Mummy,' he says,
'But I like this one, can we choose this one?'

Appendix

The following pages are excerpts from the original copies of secret police surveillance files in Romanian received from the Centre for the Study of the Archives of the Securitate (CNSAS). I translated them as the stand-alone pieces that I placed in the main body of the book. The aim of this appendix is to give a visual sense of the historical material that led to the making of these poems, and a sense of the original secret police language for those who can read Romanian.

Reading fifty, or a hundred, or just several pages of this material in one sitting has left me with whole blocks of the files, which I felt compelled to translate and respond to, or with just lines from the files that resonated with me. It is beyond the scope of this book to put in all the files from which I have taken isolated quotes.

C.B.
Stony Brook, NY,
19 February 2016

Redat din l. română
Post: -13 IBER.
Nr. file: -2
NR. 0026124

STRICT SECRET
EX. UNIC 158
DATA: -26.10.1988
INDICATIV: -1/B.I.

Exploatare la cap: ...

„BARBU"

Ora 5^{00} ob. şi soţia pleacă la serviciu. La ora 18^{10} soţia soseşte la domiciliu. După 25 minute soseşte şi ob. În cameră se înregistrează următoarele discuţii:

Soţia: - Unde ai fost?

Ob.: - La SĂFTICA. O să vină în seara asta pe la noi. Pe unde-am fost, am fost întrebat pe unde vin acasă. Pe calea ferată sau pe şosea, şi pe unde mă duc la serviciu.

Soţia: - Ei, nu mai spune!?

Ob.: - Eu am să mă duc la SAMOILĂ (şef de la Grupul de muncă) să explice despre ce este vorba, şi-am să vin cu 5^{30} (17^{30}) acasă. Ce să înţeleg din treaba asta?

Soţia: - Numai că vor să-ţi „aranjeze" ceva?

Ob.: - Dacă vrea să aranjeze ceva, de ce trebuie să dau la ăştia zvon? La să-i aranjeze; trebuie să aranjeze mai fin, ...

Soţia: - Asta ca să afle pe unde vii.

See translation of this page and excerpts from the following two pages on pages 24-25. See the poem 'Their Way', p. 26.

S.:– Ca să afle, pot să stea la pîndă o
   săptămînă și, ...
soția:– Sigur, pentru că tu n-ai pe unde merge
   la gară, decît pe partea asta.
S.:– Asta, numai a te teroriza. Asta să-nsemne.
soția:– Da, ca tu să afli.
S.:– Da, ca să le "porți de frică"? Așa zic
   eu. Că dacă ar avea de gînd să facă
   ceva, nu "vorbea".
soția:– N-are rost să să te complici, dar trebuie
   să le dai "peste nas" pururîndu-le :.– Domnule,
   am alarmat toată lumea și să știți
   că alarmez toți străinii, toate cunoștin-
   țele. Nu să interesează pe unde vin și
   pe unde plec eu la serviciu. LE spui
   asta și LE "astupi" gura. Eu dovedesc,
   nu ascea, ci sau oameni cu mine
   și mă duc la București.
      Asta nu poți să faci, pentru că sînt oa-
   meni de aci. (Dragoșești). Dacă ar veni
   un oarecare – neg Gheorghe –, să-ți spună,
   da.
S.:– Da, dar nici pe ăla nu poți să-l "bagi",
   pentru că omul vrea să-ți "facă un
   bine", și tu îi faci rău.
      Cînd să vrea să aranjeze ceva, ca să
   mă supărimul.
soția:– Da.
S.:– Asta zic eu. Să pună niște huligani
   să mă bată.

Soţia:- Da.

Ob.:- Toate să pună bulgării, dintre ai lor, de la Bucureşti.

Soţia:- De azi înainte, mergem împreună la gară. De acolo vii cu soţul şi te aştept.

Ştie şi soţia de treaba asta?

Ob.:- Da.

Soţia:- Şi spui lui Bacin, că de mult te obsedeaza ideea asta. Nu-i spui de unde ştii. Şi spui că-ţi este teamă şi tremură când pleci pe timp.

Nu.- în continuare ei pleacă în altă cameră, de unde discuţia / devine neinteligibilă. ??

*   *   *

Ora 19¹⁰, la ob. soseşte un cet. şi o cetă (se pare că e soţia şi soţul ei). Se discută în altă cameră, discuţiile fiind neinteligibile.

Ora 20⁰⁰ se camută soţia cu altă soţie. Se şi plecată în cafea.

La 20¹⁵ soseşte în cameră ob. şi soţul acestei soţie. Ob. dă drumul funcţionării aparatului de radio pe lungimea de undă a postului «Europa Liberă». Aparatul funcţionează la un volum (sonor) puternic. Nu se înţelege ce se discută.

— x —

Ora 20⁴⁵ la ob. soseşte un cet. soţia şi ob. pleacă în altă cameră pentru a discuta cu cet.

În cameră cu mijlc. T.O. rămâne soţia şi soţul ei.

Ora 21³⁰ ob. şi soţia vin în cameră şi stau la masă.

See translation of this page and the next page on p.28;
see poem on p.29, 'Legends'.

R:- bine.

——— x ———

M.I. - menționez faptul că, convorbirea este legendată. Nu mai pot înregistrări de acest gen, cu ideea că să se lase impresia că ob. are la dispoziție propriul său remustrări. (aluzie la preocupările sale ale ob-lui, cu privire la atentat asupra integrității corporale).

——— x ———

Redat:- P. A.
27.10.1988.

— BARBU —

de la ora 22⁰⁰, obiectivul ascultă în cameră știrile de la postul de radio "Europa liberă". Soția se este preocupată de lucrul la mașină. La ora 22²⁵, obiectivul caută să-l adoarmă pe Cătălin, spunându-i o poveste. cu ceva imaginar, acțiunea petrecându-se în occident, cu o viață îndestulată și fără griji, o țară cu lămâi și portocali...
Soția: ...lasă că e bine și aici cu mere, pere, păruni...
ob: ...Eu am citit mult revista Lumea și am văzut că "acolo" în

See translation of this and next page on page 30.
See the poem 'There', p. 31.

țările cu ritm ridicat de dezvoltare,
problema mâncării e ceva banal,
se găsește de toate... Dar unde este mai
bine?! Acolo unde găsești o bucată
de cașcaval sau aici la o bucată
de pâine neagră?...
Știu: E bine și aici!...

———— x ————

24.02.88
Redat: T. G.

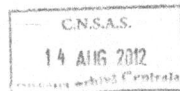

«BARBU»

Ora 5⁵ ... faurbra ... Urmează discuțiile suprasolicitate, B. îi spune lui CARMEN: "– Tu să fii foarte atentă, pentru că vei fi urmărită."
Carmen:– Nu-mi pasă. Eu dacă eram avocatul tău la proces, te scăpam de închisoare.
B.:– Știu asta. Dacă nu tu ai știut că am făcut închisoare degeaba.
Carmen:– Sigur că da.

See translation of this page on p.32.
See the poem 'October 24, 1988', p.33.

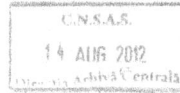

„BARBU"

Ora 17⁴⁰ ob. soseşte la domiciliu, de la locul de muncă. În cameră şi pune soţiei: „- CARMEN n-o să ia la facultate. Nu că ea n-ar fi deşteaptă şi ştie carte, ci că nu trebuie să reuşească. Se amvă în politică."

Soţia: - Din cauza ta. Noi n-am vrut să ştie nimeni unde dă examen, dar pnuă la urmă o să afle.

ob.: - Cum aţi ieşit pe poartă şi v-aţi urcat în tren, securitatea este pe urmele voastre.

Soţia: - O să-mi dau seama dacă ştie aşa.

————— x —————

După aceste afirmaţii, ei iese în curte, la treburi gospodăreşti: - soţia la bucătărie, iar ob. în pivniţă.

————— x —————

Ora 20³⁰, ob. vine în cameră cu aparatul de radio. Dă drumul funcţionării aparatului şi pnuă la ora 22⁰⁰ el audiază ştirile tran-

The translation of this and next page appears on p.34.
See poem 'Letter to "P.A."' on p.35.

busse de postul de radio stiri în l. română
a VOCEA AMERICII".

În cameră se află și soția, dar nu s-au
înregistrat comentarii.

— x —

Redat: – A.A.
14. 07. 1988.

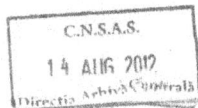

Nr. crt.	S P E C I F I C A R E	Nr. zilelor ce se scad	Nr. zilelor ce se adaugă	Nr. zilelor de executat
1	Are de executat . . . . . *11 ani*			*4015*
2	Prin decretul nr. ————— pedeapsa a fost redusă la ————— egală cu			
3	A executat arest preventiv de la ————— pînă la ———— ceea ce reprezintă			
4	De la *7.03.965* pînă la (data întocmirii procesului-verbal) *30.11.965* a executat din pedeapsă	*269*		*3746*
5	De la data ————— pînă la ————— muncind în condițiile dec. 72/950 un număr de ——— zile, urmează să se scadă			
6	Muncind în condițiile dec. 336/57 de la ————— pînă la ————— un număr de——— zile, cu aplicarea cuantumului prevăzut în decret, urmează ca			
7	Muncind în condițiile dec. 720/956 de la *01 X 965* pînă la *30.11 965* un număr de *43* zile, cu aplicarea cuantumului prevăzut în regulament urmează ca	*33*		*3713*
8	Datorită relei comportări*) *nu se socotește beneficiul de la pct. 6.* în urma cărui fapt		*33*	*3746*
9	Dînd dovezi temeinice de îndreptare se repun în vigoare procesele verbale nr. ————— urmînd să se scadă			

10 Față de cele de mai sus, comisia constată că (motivarea și concluzia) *din nutrul CR BURGAN IOAN mai are de executat din pedeapsă nu nu mai de 3746 zile.*

————— Drept pentru care am încheiat prezentul proces-verbal —————

PREȘEDINTE,   Secretar,   Membrii,

*) Se va completa de la caz la caz cu formula :
„nu se socotește beneficiul de la pct. 6 (pct. 7 D. 336/957).
„se anulează procesul verbal nr. —————   ".

NOTA: La „specificare" se vor completa numai spațiile cu linii, iar acolo unde sînt puncte completarea se va face în coloana respectivă.

Data *10.12.965*
Am luat cunoștință

Condamnat,

See translation of this file on p.38.
See the poem '3746 days', p.39.

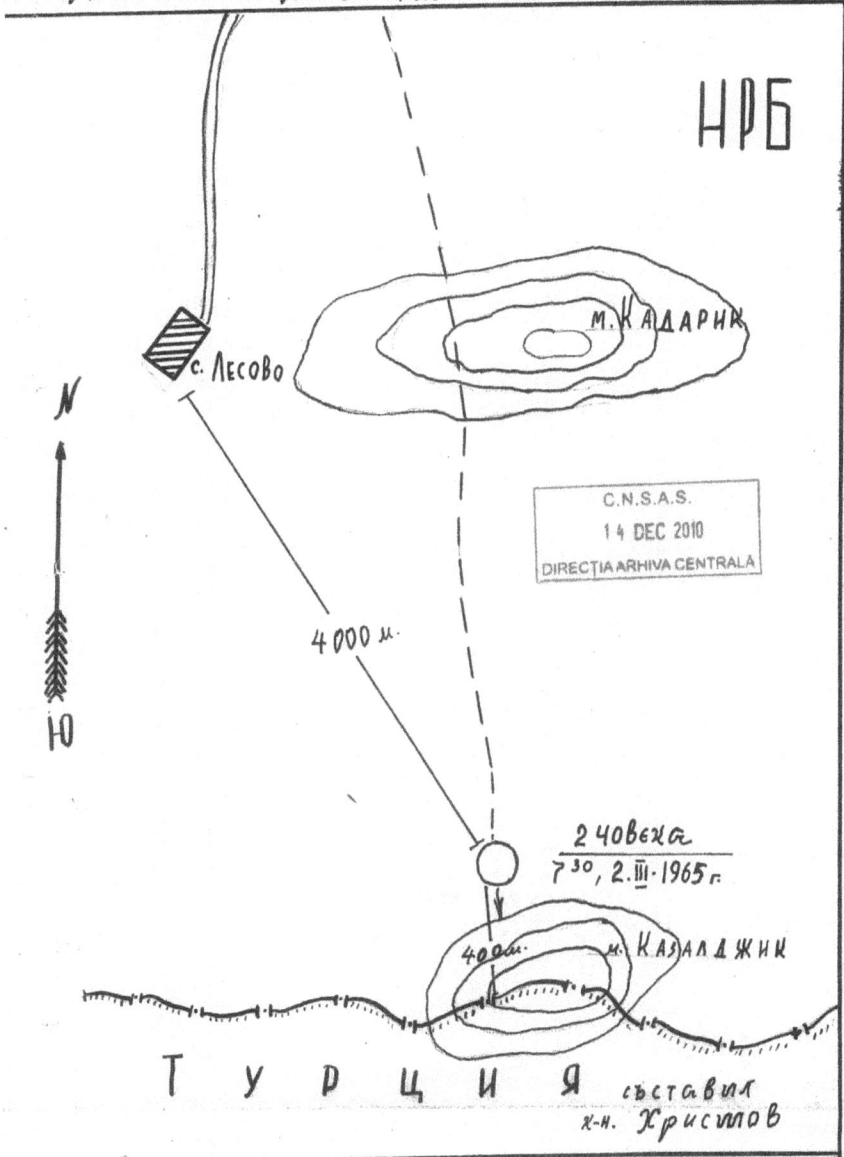

С Х Е М А

за задържането на нарушителите П█████ Т. Бнэа и БОГА ЙОН

НРБ

с. ЛЕСОВО

м. КАДАРИК

N

Ю

4 000 м.

2 чОвекa
7³⁰, 2.Ⅲ.1965 г.

400 м.   м. КАЗАЛДЖИК

Т У Р Ц И Я   съставил
х-н. Христов

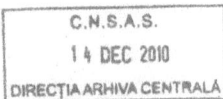

213 (212)

A D E V E R I N Ţ A
=====================
de predarea şi primirea obiectelor.

Subsemnatul Lt.colonel C▮▮▮▮ Z▮▮▮ din partea
U.M.o2866 Constanţa am predat, iar maior A▮▮▮ I▮ din partea
Dir.Regionale M.A.I.Dobrogea am primit următoarele obiecte şi
documente :

1)- 1(un)protocol(proces verbal)de cercetarea terenului
compus din două file şi anexă 4(patru) fotocopii;
2)- 1(una)raniţă turistică;
3)- 1(un)port pentru binoclu;
4)-2(două)pleduri de molton;
5)- 1(una)maşină de bărbierit;
6)- 1(una)pensulă de bărbierit;
7)- 1(un) tub pastă bărbierit;
8)- 1(una)baterie de 4,5 W;
9)- 1(una)brichetă;
1o)- 1(una)monedă metalică a 3 lei;
11)- 4(patru) monede a un leu;
12)- 6(şase) monede a 5 bani;
13)- 2(două)monede a lo bani;
14)- 1(un)dicţionar englez-romîn;
15)- 1(un)manual de limbă germană-12 pagini în stare de-
teriorară;
16)- 3(trei)bucăţi pînză obiele;
17)- 1(una)sticlă de bere cu 5o ml.spirt;
18)- 17(şaptesprezece)jumătăti de bucăţi salam vinatoresc;
19)-2(două)franzele;
2o)- 1(una)surubelniţă
Obiectele de mai sus aparţin infractorilor de
frontieră P▮▮▮ T▮▮ şi BUGAN IOAN care au trecut frontiera
din R.P.R. în R.P.B. în ziua de 21.o2.1965 ora 23,35 printre
bornele 11o-111.

..//..

See translation of this and the following page on page 40. Names other than
those of the Bugan family have been redacted. This file, along with the map on
the previous page figure in the poem 'A walk with my father on the
Iron Curtain', pp. 41-42.

Cu ocazia predării și primirii nu s-au făcut nici
un fel de obiectiuni.

Incheiat astăzi 20.03.1965 la Constanta.

DIN PARTEA U.M.o2866 CONSTANTA
  Lt.colonel,
       ss/ Z.C████████   DIN PARTEA DIR.REG.M.A.I.
                                  DOBROGEA
                                    ss/Mr.A██████ I████

www.ingramcontent.com/pod-product-compliance
Lightning Source LLC
Chambersburg PA
CBHW022206080426
42734CB00006B/567